# Follow You

When Elizabeth Thatcher followed her dream, hopped on a stage coach, and headed West to become a teacher, one of the things she took with her was her beloved journal. It was a place for her to capture her thoughts, to record moments from her daily life, and to write about what was on her heart. That journal became a treasure, for her, her loved ones, and for future generations who could get to know her through the words on those pages.

The same is true for us. There's something deeply meaningful about writing down our stories, the moments of our lives, our prayer needs, and chronicling our time spent in study and reflection with God. And on days when we're discouraged or we don't see how we're going to make it through a difficult circumstance, sitting down and re-reading our journal entries can remind us of His faithfulness in every situation. It's a gift that we can pass down to future generations.

If you haven't discovered the companion devotional book for this journal, *When God Calls the Heart: Devotions from Hope Valley*, it's based on the *When Calls the Heart* television series (and the beloved novels by Janette Oke), and written by the show's executive producer and co-creator, Brian Bird, and inspirational writer Michelle Cox. *When God Calls the Heart* contains 40 devotions that illuminate the "God-moments" from the fictional 1910 mining town of Hope Valley. The stories of faith, hope, and love from each episode will touch your soul, inspire, and encourage you with wonderful virtues and relatable life lessons.

We hope you enjoy using your *When God Calls the Heart Journal*. We're confident that by the time you fill in the last beautiful page, you'll have learned what Elizabeth Thatcher did during her years in Hope Valley. Because when God calls your heart, you can expect an adventure.

Happy writing!

Brian Bird and Michelle Cox

"You will seek me and find me

when you seek me with all your heart."

JEREMIAH 29:13 NIV

Face your fears and get outside your
comfort zones—that's the only way
impossible challenges become possible.

I can do this. We can do whatever

God calls us to do—with His help.

—Elizabeth Thatcher

You are God's beautiful creation—

a unique masterpiece

made in His image.

"For I know the plans I have for you," declares

the Lord, "plans to prosper you and not to

harm you, plans to give you hope and a future."

JEREMIAH 29:11 NIV

Persistence always beats resistance.

You, Lord, are a compassionate and
gracious God, slow to anger,
abounding in love and faithfulness.

PSALM 86:15 NIV

Trouble rides a fast horse.

Weeping may endure for a night,

But joy comes in the morning.

PSALM 30:5 NKJV

God allows the storms.

Without them, we would never

have the blessing of His provision.

Sometimes we need to trust each other,

because the truth isn't always

what it appears to be.

—Elizabeth Thatcher

God knows our strengths and weaknesses.

He smiles at our victories and stands ready

to catch us when we fall.

_____

_____

_____

_____

_____

_____

_____

_____

_____

_____

_____

_____

_____

_____

_____

_____

_____

_____

_____

_____

_____

"See, I am doing a new thing! Now it springs

up; do you not perceive it?

I am making a way in the wilderness

and streams in the wasteland."

ISAIAH 43:19 NIV

God has a plan for us in ation.
an.

The light of love restores every lost voice.

—Elizabeth Thatcher

Listen to those who love you

and have your best interests at heart.

Many are the plans in the mind of a man,

but it is the purpose of the Lord that will stand.

PROVERBS 19:21 ESV

Sometimes the best way to fix
a broken relationship is to be
the first one to be the peacemaker.

You are enough.

In fact, more than enough...

because God says so.

"For where your treasure is,

there your heart will be also."

MATTHEW 6:21 NKJV

The decisions we make each day will determine
if we'll reach the end of our days with a bitter
or better treasure. Better is always better.

In the day of trouble

he will keep me safe in his dwelling;

he will hide me in the shelter of his sacred tent

and set me high upon a rock.

PSALM 27:5 NIV

Sometimes the only way we can find
a new purpose, or reach a new blessing God
has in store for us, is to be willing to turn loose
of things that are precious to us and take
a step outside our comfort zone.

There is a time for everything,

and a season for every activity under the heavens:

ECCLESIASTES 3:1 NIV

It doesn't always cost a lot

to make a difference in someone's life.

I've always found that the best way

to wash away worry is through prayer.

—MOLLY SULLIVAN

Quitting and failure in times of challenge are
never an option. When we take on that attitude,
we can be an unstoppable force for good.

If any of you lacks wisdom, you should ask
God, who gives generously to all without
finding fault, and it will be given to you.

JAMES 1:5 NIV

People can discourage us and circumstances
can temporarily defeat us, but God never wants
us to give up on the dreams He has for us.

Be anxious for nothing, but in everything
by prayer and supplication, with thanksgiving,
let your requests be made known to God.

PHILIPPIANS 4:6 NKJV

The antidote for worry is to take action:
Turn it over to God! And then sit back
and relax. He's got it, and He doesn't
need your advice on what to do next.

This is the confidence we have in approaching

God: that if we ask anything according to his will,

he hears us.

I JOHN 5:14 NIV

Kindness, generosity, and tender loving care

heals a hurting heart every time.

Sometimes we spend so much time
searching for the answers, we don't realize
they are right under our nose.

—CHARLES KENSINGTON

He sometimes doesn't answer our prayers in the way we expect, but God grants us what we need.

"Have I not commanded you? Be strong and of good

courage; do not be afraid, nor be dismayed,

for the LORD your God is with you wherever you go."

JOSHUA 1:9 NKJV

_____

_____

_____

_____

_____

_____

_____

_____

_____

_____

_____

_____

_____

_____

_____

_____

_____

_____

_____

_____

_____

_____

_____

_____

God has given you a specific purpose and

calling to fulfill with your skills and talents.

_____
_____
_____
_____
_____
_____
_____
_____
_____
_____
_____
_____
_____
_____
_____
_____
_____
_____
_____
_____
_____
_____
_____
_____

From the time we're young, people assume
we're not capable of certain things.
Sometimes we just need to prove 'em wrong.

—JACK THORNTON

_____

_____

_____

_____

_____

_____

_____

_____

_____

_____

_____

_____

_____

_____

_____

_____

_____

_____

_____

_____

_____

_____

_____

_____

_____

God tells us to bring our burdens to Him,

but it's apparent most of us are slow learners

in that department.

Wait for the Lord;

be strong and take heart and wait for the Lord.

Psalm 27:14 niv

When you feel no one gets you, when no one
will take the time to really listen to you, just tell
God what's on your heart. He will listen;
He will comfort you; He will give you peace
about your situation.

To all who did receive him, to those who
believed in his name, he gave the right
to become children of God.

JOHN 1:12 NIV

Sometimes our biggest obstacles

are inside our own heads.

Because of the Lord's great love we are not

consumed, for his compassions never fail.

They are new every morning;

great is your faithfulness.

LAMENTATIONS 3:22–23 NIV

When life gets hard,

the best place to be is on our knees.

When you truly love someone,

all you want is for them to be happy.

—ABIGAIL STANTON

No matter what you've done

or what has happened in your life,

God will never give up on you.

_____

_____

_____

_____

_____

_____

_____

_____

_____

_____

_____

_____

_____

_____

_____

_____

_____

_____

_____

_____

_____

"When you pass through the waters, I will be
with you; and when you pass through the rivers,
they will not sweep over you. When you walk
through the fire, you will not be burned;
the flames will not set you ablaze."

ISAIAH 43:2 NIV

Grievances hurt us more

than those we hold them against.

It doesn't matter who started it.
What's important is that we all learn
to treat each other with kindness.

—ELIZABETH THATCHER

The key is, don't tell God what *you* want;

ask Him what *He* wants.

Be kind to one another,

tenderhearted, forgiving one another,

even as God in Christ forgave you.

EPHESIANS 4:32 NKJV

You have the power to choose
how you live every day of your life.

Be strong and do not give up,

for your work will be rewarded.

2 Chronicles 15:7 NIV

Don't back your way into prayer.

Make it your first choice.

Sometimes our smallest actions

lead to our biggest victories.

—Elizabeth Thatcher

_____

_____

_____

_____

_____

_____

_____

_____

_____

_____

_____

_____

_____

_____

_____

_____

_____

_____

_____

_____

_____

_____

_____

_____

_____

God is your shelter in the storms of your

circumstances and a refuge of understanding

in the sea of chaotic relationships.

The heart of man plans his way,

but the Lord establishes his steps.

PROVERBS 16:9 ESV

When God writes a new chapter for our lives,
it's not because He wants to take something away
or wants to say "no." It's because He wants us to
say the "better yes" to what He has waiting for us.

"Do to others as you would like them

to do to you."

LUKE 6:31 NLT

_____

_____

_____

_____

_____

_____

_____

_____

_____

_____

_____

_____

_____

_____

_____

_____

_____

_____

_____

_____

God's way of dealing with His children in
all their moods is to show them love. For us,
sometimes that means sacrificing our own
needs in order to love the unlovable.

_____

_____

_____

_____

_____

_____

_____

_____

_____

_____

_____

_____

_____

_____

_____

_____

_____

_____

_____

_____

_____

"Then you will call upon Me
and go and pray to Me,
and I will listen to you."

JEREMIAH 29:12 NKJV

You have infinite worth

because you are a child of the King.

_____

_____

_____

_____

_____

_____

_____

_____

_____

_____

_____

_____

_____

_____

_____

_____

_____

_____

_____

_____

_____

_____

_____

_____

I believe that there's a reason for every fear

we face and every hardship we suffer—

and it's to make us all stronger people.

—ELIZABETH THATCHER

When faithful people pray in earnest,

big things can happen.

Let each of you look out not only for his own

interests, but also for the interests of others.

PHILIPPIANS 2:4 NKJV

Great joy can be found in giving

and doing for others.

Do not remember the former things,

Nor consider the things of old.

ISAIAH 43:18 NKJV

The Author of all things writes

the stories of our lives.

_____

_____

_____

_____

_____

_____

_____

_____

_____

_____

_____

_____

_____

_____

_____

_____

_____

_____

_____

_____

_____

_____

For what is life but a bittersweet mix of sadness,

wonderment, hope, and joy?

—ELIZABETH THATCHER

God will never misconstrue you.

He knows your heart, your motives.

"A new commandment I give to you,

that you love one another."

JOHN 13:34 NKJV

Love paired with compassion and action can comfort a wounded heart, revive a defeated spirit, and inspire someone to keep going.

We are hard-pressed on every side,

yet not crushed; we are perplexed,

but not in despair; persecuted,

but not forsaken; struck down,

but not destroyed.

2 Corinthians 4:8-9 NKJV

There's nothing in the Bible that includes

the words, "… and then God failed me."

He heals the brokenhearted

And binds up their wounds.

Instead of writing people off as lost causes,

we need to pray that God will

miraculously change them

When I am afraid,

I will put my trust in You.

PSALM 56:3 NASB